## LUIGI PIRANDELLO

Born in Sicily in 1867, Pirandello went to university in Palermo
and Rome and took a doctorate in Bonn, before settling into the
café-bohemian literary life of Rome in the 1890s. In 1894 he
married the beautiful daughter of his father's business associate,
but after bearing three children her already fragile mental stability
was undermined by the financial ruin of both her father and father-
in-law. Pirandello supported his family by taking a university
lecturing post – and by writing. Most of his best-known works
were written in the shadows of his wife's increasingly dangerous
condition.

He first established his reputation with short stories, novels and
two philosophical works. Playwriting came fairly late in his
career, but it was his plays which won him an international
reputation. Amongst the best-known outside Italy are *Right You
Are, If You Think So!* (1917), *The Rules of the Game* (1918), *Six
Characters in Search of an Author* (1921), which provoked uproar
when first staged in Rome but soon came to be seen as seminal,
helped by an enormously successful production in Paris in 1924,
*Naked* (1922), *Henry IV* (1922), *The Man with the Flower in his
Mouth* (1923), *As You Desire Me* (1936) and *The Mountain Giants*,
produced a year after his death in Rome in 1936. He won the
Nobel Prize for Literature in 1934.

## NICHOLAS WRIGHT

Nicholas Wright's plays include *Treetops* and *One Fine Day*
(Riverside Studios), *The Gorky Brigade* (Royal Court), *The
Crimes of Vautrin* (Joint Stock), *The Custom of the Country* and
*The Desert Air* (RSC) and *Mrs Klein* (National Theatre, West End,
New York). Screenplays include adaptations of novels by Patrick
Hamilton, Doris Lessing, Josef Skvorecky, Armistead Maupin and
Ford Madox Ford. His writing about the theatre includes *99 Plays,*
a personal view of playwriting from Aeschylus to the present.
For the National Theatre he has written versions of *Six Characters
in Search of an Author* and *John Gabriel Borkman.* He was the
first director of the Royal Court's Theatre Upstairs, was joint
Artistic Director of the Royal Court in the 1970s and is now
an Associate Director of the National Theatre.

## Other Titles in this Series

# LUIGI PIRANDELLO

# Naked

*a new version by*
Nicholas Wright

*from a literal translation by*
Gaynor McFarlane

**NICK HERN BOOKS**
LONDON

**A Nick Hern Book**

*Naked* first published in Great Britain in this version
as an original paperback in 1998 by Nick Hern Books Limited,
14 Larden Road, London W3 7ST

Typeset by Country Setting, Woodchurch, Kent TN26 3TB
Printed in England by Athenæum Press Ltd,
Gateshead, Tyne and Wear

ISBN 185459 339 0

A CIP catalogue record for this book is available from
the British Library

This new version by Nicholas Wright of Luigi Pirandello's
*Naked* was first performed at the Almeida Theatre, London,
on 12 February 1998. The cast, in order of appearance, was
as follows:

| | |
|---|---|
| ERSILIA DREI | Juliette Binoche |
| FRANCO LASPIGA | Ben Daniels |
| GROTTI | Kevin McNally |
| LUDOVICO NOTA | Oliver Ford Davies |
| ALFREDO CANTAVALLE | David Sibley |
| SIGNORIA ONORIA | Anita Reeves |
| EMMA | Romy Baskerville |

*Direction*   Jonathan Kent
*Design*   Paul Brown
*Lighting*   Mark Henderson
*Music*   Jonathan Dove
*Sound*   John A. Leonard
*Voice*   Patsy Rodenberg
*Literal Translation*   Gaynor McFarlane
*Casting*   Wendy Brazington
*Assistant Director*   Tom Yarwood

*Production Photographer*   Ivan Kyncl
*Production Manager*   Paul Clay
*Company Stage Manager*   Rupert Carlile
*Stage Manager*   Lisa Buckley
*Deputy Stage Manager*   Debbie Green
*Assistant Stage Manager*   Kathy Anders

*Chief Technician*   James Crout
*Technicians*   Helen Holbrook, Paul Skelton
*Master Carpenter*   Craig Emerson
*Costume Supervisor*   Jane Hamilton
*Wardrobe Supervisor*   Susannah Gorgeous

**Characters**

LUDOVICO NOTA, *a novelist*

ERSILIA DREI

SIGNORA ONORIA, *a landlady*

ALFREDO CANTAVALLE, a *journalist*

FRANCO LASPIGA, *formerly a Naval Lieutenant*

EMMA, *the maid*

CONSUL GROTTI

*Place:* Rome.

*Time:* Summer of 1922

## Act One

*A large room in a rented apartment. This is the study of* LUDO-
VICO NOTA, *novelist. A few pieces of antique furniture –*
NOTA's *own – stand out in contrast to the cheap junk supplied
by* SIGNORA ONORIA, *his landlady.*

*The room is dark: the narrowness of the street outside and the
height of the houses mean that very little daylight enters. But the
window admits an enormous amount of noise. We hear the din of
cars, lorries, bicycle bells, the blare of horns, the judder of
motorbikes, the clamour of voices and the cries of street-vendors.*

*The room is empty. Then the apartment-door opens and* ERSILIA
DREI *comes in. She's a beautiful young woman of just over
twenty, respectably but shabbily dressed. These surroundings are
new to her. She looks round the room, perhaps waiting for
somebody else to enter.*

*Now* LUDOVICO NOTA *comes in, stuffing his wallet back into
his inside pocket. He's a handsome, convivial man, past fifty.*

LUDOVICO. Here we are!

*He sees her standing.*

Please . . . ! Sit down! This is your home now.

*She sits. There's a sudden noise from outside.* LUDOVICO
*looks up in irritation.*

That window.

*He goes over to close it. As he winds it closed.*

When it's open, the noise is deafening. But if one leaves it
closed for any length of time, the room develops a sort of
sticky, swamp-like atmosphere. I don't know which of the two
is worse. Now won't you . . . ?

*Pause.*

Won't you remove your hat?

*She does. Slowly, she puts it down. He watches. Unexpectedly,*
SIGNORA ONORIA *appears in the bedroom door, a bundle of
dirty sheets under her arm.*

ONORIA. I'm coming through.

LUDOVICO. Good God! What were you doing in there?

ONORIA. I read your note. And so I've changed the sheets. I don't know why you . . .

*She sees* ERSILIA.

Ah. I see.

*To* LUDOVICO.

You and I had better have a talk. I'll take these out and then . . .

LUDOVICO. Quite so! Let's get rid of those disgusting objects.

ONORIA. *Disgusting?*

LUDOVICO. Yes. You said yourself, you wanted to remove them.

ONORIA. What about *that* disgusting object? What about *her?*

LUDOVICO. This young lady is my guest. If you continue to insult her . . .

ONORIA. What if I do? What then?

*Pause.*

I'll be back.

*She goes.*

LUDOVICO (*to* ERSILIA). Sad, disappointed creature. She'll come round. She'll have to. I'm standing firm on this. My home is yours. Now, if you'd . . .

ONORIA *appears in the doorway.*

ONORIA. Your *home?* You're a *lodger.* This is a decent house, and . . . !

LUDOVICO. Decent? Is it? You amaze me.

ONORIA. I let out rooms because I have to. It doesn't mean I'm not respectable. And I won't have tenants bringing their sluts on to the premises.

LUDOVICO. Bringing their . . .

*He explodes.*

Stupid, ignorant woman!

ONORIA. Sleep with her somewhere else! Not here! I won't allow it!

LUDOVICO. Can you not see she's ill?

ONORIA *is taken aback by this.*

ONORIA. Ill?

LUDOVICO. She was discharged from hospital this morning. I've offered to lend her my rooms for a couple of days. And you can't stop me!

ONORIA. Yes I can. She's not the tenant.

LUDOVICO. And if she were my sister? Or an aunt?

ONORIA. She could find a hotel.

LUDOVICO. For a couple of nights? That's ridiculous!

ONORIA. But she *isn't* your sister. Nor your . . .

LUDOVICO. I was speaking hypothetically. Naturally I shall sleep elsewhere. Well?

ONORIA. You'll have to ask. Politely.

LUDOVICO. I'm *invariably* polite.

ONORIA. No comments about the swamp-like smell?

LUDOVICO. None. You have my word of honour. It will go unmentioned. (*Furious.*) Along with all your other moist and fetid odours!

ONORIA. Why don't you leave then, if you hate it here?

LUDOVICO. I will!

ONORIA. Are you giving me notice?

LUDOVICO. Yes! I'll leave on Friday! Well . . . at the end of the month!

ONORIA. I'll hold you to that!

LUDOVICO. Please do!

> LUDOVICO *watches her go. Turns to* ERSILIA.

And off she hops, the great she-toad, to spread the news to her fellow amphibians. I'm sorry. You'd barely walked in the door before it started. Can you forgive me?

ERSILIA. There's nothing to forgive. It was me who caused it.

LUDOVICO. You? . . . no, that was mere routine . . . she and I have been at war for the past twelve months. I can't shake her off. She's like some parasitical growth. And now you're cruelly disappointed. You arrive at a novelist's home. You anticipate civilised talk, good food, the scurry of servants . . . ?

ERSILIA. No. I think it's sad, though, that a famous man like you . . .

LUDOVICO. Enough of that! We've two weeks left in which to find . . . in the first place, somewhere quieter. Some tree-lined street, with a park nearby. We'll buy some simple furniture . . . things for the kitchen . . . whatever you want.

ERSILIA. Are you doing all this for *me?*

LUDOVICO. Oh, I'd leave anyway. I'm a nomad . . . never happier than when folding up my tent . . . but writing to *you* . . . to offer you shelter . . . *that* was inspired! The swamp lies dark and still . . . the air is humid . . . flies hang motionless . . . then a breath . . . a puff of wind . . . one is refreshed . . . renewed!

ERSILIA. Thank you.

LUDOVICO. Thank *you,* for accepting the little I have to give.

ERSILIA. How can you say that? You've saved my life. I was desperate. I didn't even know where I was going to sleep. Then I got your letter and . . . I felt so embarrassed.

LUDOVICO. Because . . . ?

ERSILIA. Because I'd heard so much about you.

LUDOVICO. Let's not allow my modest reputation to stand between us.

ERSILIA. When I realised that a man like you had taken pity on me . . .

LUDOVICO. Not pity, no. I felt an interest. No, it was more than that.

*He stares at her for a moment.*

I was reading the paper. And I was half-way through the story about you when I felt a . . . jolt. A thrill of recognition. I couldn't explain it. It was like those moments when I'm writing . . . when, out of the air, a face or a name or a theme emerges. And it's beautiful and unexpected and it changes everything. That's how I felt about you.

ERSILIA. Do you mean you want to *write* about me?

LUDOVICO. Plunder your life for a work of fiction? Certainly not!

ERSILIA. But if you did . . . if all the things that have happened to me could be turned into something better . . .

LUDOVICO. You mean . . . a novel?

ERSILIA. Yes! I'd feel so proud if that could happen. And if *you* were to write it . . .

LUDOVICO *makes a sudden, dramatic movement of renunciation.*

LUDOVICO. Then I give up!

ERSILIA. Why?

LUDOVICO. Because, my dear . . . you have reminded me of my age.

ERSILIA. By what I said?

LUDOVICO. By what you assumed. There are stories in print, and stories in life. I offer you, not the tuppence coloured of fiction, but the honest penny plain of a human relationship. I stretch out a hand, hoping that you might brush it with your lips. And what do you do? You place a pen between my fingers and tell me to start writing.

ERSILIA. But it's too soon for me to . . . (*get involved with anyone*).

LUDOVICO. Too soon for lips? Of course. But later?

ERSILIA. No!

LUDOVICO *takes a moment to absorb this plain refusal.*

LUDOVICO. Then we've much to learn. You imagined that I was drawn to you for artistic reasons. I had allowed my thoughts to wander further. Now I'm hurt. *You* would be hurt, I think, to realise that an experienced writer . . . not quite a veteran . . . but a man with some grasp of the tricks of the trade, scarcely needed to write to you . . . still less to play sentry at the door of the hospital . . . merely to research your story. Because I only had to read it in my morning paper for an entire novel to spring to life.

ERSILIA. How?

LUDOVICO. I saw it . . . rich in detail, glowing with colour! The Levant! The sea and a beach-front villa. Flat roof . . . you, the governess, padding the corridors . . . siesta-hour . . . then a cry . . . a tiny body falls to the ground. Dismissal . . . arrival in Rome . . . betrayal. I saw it all!

ERSILIA. And what was I like?

*She indicates herself.*

Was I like this?

LUDOVICO *smiles.*

LUDOVICO. No.

ERSILIA. So you thought of a novel . . . and the story was mine . . . but the woman was someone else?

LUDOVICO. Exactly.

ERSILIA. And she was different from me?

LUDOVICO. She was a different person.

ERSILIA. Oh, I don't understand!

LUDOVICO. What don't you . . . (*understand*)?

ERSILIA. Why are you even *bothering* with me? If I'm not *her* . . . if the story in the paper made you think of somebody else completely . . .

*She breaks off, confused.*

LUDOVICO. Well?

ERSILIA. Then I shouldn't be here.

LUDOVICO (*playful*). No, no! We'll let the other woman go, and keep the *real* one.

ERSILIA. But she's *also* me!

LUDOVICO. She doesn't matter! Let's forget about her. Let's forget about you as you *were*. Let us imagine a new, unprecedented you . . . a woman whose life has only just started. Can you do that?

ERSILIA. You mean . . . not myself . . . and not the woman you imagined . . . but a third one?

LUDOVICO. Yes. The woman you will be.

ERSILIA. But I've never been anyone.

LUDOVICO. Never been . . . ?

ERSILIA. Never.

LUDOVICO. But you're yourself!

ERSILIA. Who's *that*?

LUDOVICO. You're an . . . exceptionally beautiful young woman.

ERSILIA. I'm not. And what if I were . . . what good would it do me?

LUDOVICO. I wondered that too . . . and then it struck me . . . that she might *exploit* her beauty.

ERSILIA. What?

LUDOVICO. The hotel bedroom . . . late evening . . . rent due, purse empty . . . she stares in the mirror . . . then, impetuously, she paints a slash of scarlet across her mouth . . .

ERSILIA. Is that what they said in the paper?

LUDOVICO. No, but . . .

*He stops. Thrilled.*

Do you mean, it's *true?*

ERSILIA *nods.*

I knew it! Later that night, she sidles down the stairs into the darkened street. Walks into the crowd . . .

ERSILIA. Yes.

LUDOVICO. Somebody stops. Looks back. A stranger.

*Pause.* ERSILIA *covers her face.*

And then?

ERSILIA. Afterwards . . . I didn't know how to ask him . . .

LUDOVICO. For the money?

*She nods.*

So . . . only the shame. And the self-disgust.

ERSILIA *sobs.*

Don't cry.

*He puts an arm round her to comfort her.*

ERSILIA. Don't touch me. I want to go.

LUDOVICO. Why?

ERSILIA. I've told you too much about myself.

LUDOVICO. But I knew already.

ERSILIA. *How?*

LUDOVICO. Intuition. It always arrives at truth.

ERSILIA. I'm so ashamed.

*There's a squeal of brakes, a blare of horns and a crash from the street below. Shouts, cries and dire threats. Meanwhile.*

LUDOVICO. No, no, my dear, there's nothing to be ashamed of . . .

*He stops.*

Oh, this is intolerable.

ERSILIA. It's an accident.

*The noise increases.* ONORIA *appears at the door.*

ONORIA. A man's been crushed against the wall! Right under the window!

*She opens the window.* LUDOVICO *and* ERSILIA *go to look. The noise from the street dominates the stage. A car has collided with a lorry. In swerving, it crushed an old man against the wall. He is now dying, perhaps already dead. Above the confusion and the shouting, an ambulance can be heard arriving. Once the ambulance-bearers have collected the victim, the ambulance will be heard leaving at full speed for the hospital. Meanwhile, voices are heard giving replays of the accident and calling for help, doctors and attention. The action below is reflected by the watchers above.*

ONORIA. Look, he's moving. Poor old . . .

*She sees the driver of the car.*

That's the driver! Stop him! That's right, hang on to him! Don't let him go!

*She shouts down.*

Lies, all lies! He squashed him like a hedgehog!

LUDOVICO. Some old labourer, by the look of him.

*To* ONORIA.

Close the window.

ONORIA. Not yet, not yet. They're putting him on the stretcher. Careful!

*She closes the window.*

Do you think he's dead?

LUDOVICO. Either that, or . . . God, what a sight. I cannot believe he'll last the journey. What happened exactly?

ONORIA. I'll go and ask.

*She goes out.*

ERSILIA. How horrible!

LUDOVICO. That street's a public scandal. Blocked drains. Mud up to one's ankles. Cars, trucks, barrows . . . they even allow a market, of all absurdities.

ERSILIA. The street. Oh God, the street.

LUDOVICO. What a lesson for the artist. One struggles to reach a higher plane . . . yet always, the street is there . . . the mud, the noise, the blank faces, the repulsive intimacies. I plan the perfect story. Then the blare of a horn intrudes. The scream of brakes, and a man lies dying. What then would my story amount to . . . if I were he?

*He looks at* ERSILIA.

But why am I telling you? You lived in a house where death came suddenly. With the fall of a child to a sun-baked pavement.

*Pause.*

ERSILIA. You work. You do what they pay you to do. And that's what you are. At night, they put you away, like a coat on a hook or a stick in the hallstand. And it's so frightening. You ask yourself, is this all that I am? Am I honestly . . . truly . . . nothing?

*Pause*

Just now . . . when that man was crushed . . . I looked . . . at *that*. At that *thing*. In the street. I thought, that's what it's like. To have no meaning.

*Pause*

I sat in the park. And everything around me was like a dream. The trees, the benches. Then a couple walked past and they looked right through me. As though I didn't exist. And I couldn't bear it. I couldn't bear being nothing.

LUDOVICO. But you weren't. How could I invent you, if you didn't exist?

ERSILIA. Do you think I'm making it up?

LUDOVICO. I mean that in *you*, I found a springboard for my imagination. And it wasn't just me. You're famous. They're talking about you on the radio. Newspapers have headlines about you. How can you not exist, when that's the case?

*Satisfied, he starts busying himself with something he's prepared for her arrival: a bottle of wine, perhaps and some biscuits.*

ERSILIA. Have you got them?

LUDOVICO. What?

ERSILIA. The newspapers.

LUDOVICO. I'm sure they're somewhere.

ERSILIA. Find them!

LUDOVICO. Aren't you afraid they might upset you?

ERSILIA. No! I want to know what they said.

LUDOVICO. No doubt they said whatever you told them.

ERSILIA. But I don't remember . . . Find them!

LUDOVICO. Easier said than done . . .

*He glances around: papers, manuscripts and magazines are scattered everywhere in no definable order.*

I'm not a systematic person . . . why don't we look together, later on?

ERSILIA. Was it a big story?

LUDOVICO. Big? The first to break had three full columns. Summer, you know, what's called the silly season . . .

ERSILIA. What did they say about *him*?

LUDOVICO. They said he left you for another woman.

ERSILIA. No . . . the other.

LUDOVICO. Your employer, you mean? The consul?

ERSILIA. Did it *say* he was a consul?

LUDOVICO. Yes. Our consul in Smyrna.

*She's appalled.*

ERSILIA. Oh God! They promised not to.

LUDOVICO (*worldly*). And you believed them?

ERSILIA. Yes! They had their story! They didn't have to print the details! What did they say about him?

LUDOVICO. They said that after the child had died . . .

ERSILIA. Oh, the child . . . my darling . . . my little angel!

LUDOVICO. . . . . they said he treated you abominably.

ERSILIA. Not him! It was his wife.

LUDOVICO. But surely he was implicated?

ERSILIA. No! He wasn't! It was only her.

LUDOVICO. Still . . . that was bad enough. From what I gather. She sounds a monster.

ERSILIA. She was. But small. And thin. With yellow skin, like a dried-up lemon.

LUDOVICO. I saw her larger than that . . . with eyebrows joining up in the middle.

ERSILIA. She's like I said.

LUDOVICO. Well, you would know . . . although she *should* be large, to form a contrast with the tiny baby.

ERSILIA (*since the baby was large for her age*). Tiny? Mimmetta!

LUDOVICO. I called her Irma.

ERSILIA. Mimmetta. A big soft child with chubby legs and golden hair. She loved me. She loved me more than anyone else in the world.

LUDOVICO. So the mother was jealous.

ERSILIA. She was. Mostly because of that. That's why she took revenge. You know the young man . . . ? The one you mentioned . . . ?

LUDOVICO. The lieutenant . . . ?

ERSILIA. Yes. It was she who brought us together. It was his last night on shore. She made certain the house was empty. He and I ate in the garden . . . the palm trees . . . the smell of the honeysuckle . . . it was like being drugged.

LUDOVICO. The sound of the waves, the starry night . . .

ERSILIA. If only I'd not given in to him . . .

LUDOVICO. No! If only she'd not trapped you! Then . . . ?

ERSILIA. Next day, he told her he was going to marry me. She seemed delighted. But when he left, she changed. She blamed me for everything. When Mimmetta died, she even blamed me for that.

LUDOVICO. Though it was she who'd sent you out of the house on an errand?

ERSILIA. Why do you say that?

LUDOVICO. I must have read it.

ERSILIA. In the paper?

LUDOVICO. Isn't it what you said?

ERSILIA. I don't remember.

LUDOVICO. No doubt the journalist made it up. To underline the harshness of your dismissal. She sent you back to Rome, but refused to pay for the journey. Is *that* correct?

ERSILIA. Yes.

LUDOVICO. The price of a boat-train ticket against the death of a
child . . .

ERSILIA. She wanted more than that. She wanted my wages
back. If she hadn't been so worried about what might come
out, she'd . . .

LUDOVICO. What?

ERSILIA *is uneasy.*

ERSILIA. Nothing. I wish I hadn't told them that. Do you know
what I'm thinking about now? The journey home. All the way,
I felt that my little dead girl was with me. As though she'd
followed me on to the boat. As though she'd left her cruel
parents to stay by the side of the only friend she had. And then
I lost her . . . the night I went down into the street . . .

LUDOVICO. But could the lieutenant not at least have helped
you? Didn't you look for him?

ERSILIA *shrugs.*

ERSILIA. I didn't know where he lived. I used to write to him
Poste Restante. I went to the Naval Ministry, but they said he'd
resigned his commission.

LUDOVICO. You should have tracked him down.

ERSILIA. I'm not a fighter.

LUDOVICO. But he'd promised to marry you!

ERSILIA. Yes! And then they told me he was marrying another
woman. Where could I go? What could I do? Sit on the corner
and beg? The only peace I had in the next three days, was
when I was sitting in the park with the bottle of poison in my
hand. When I thought of the child. When I thought that, if I
died, I might meet her again.

LUDOVICO. And now the nightmare's over.

ERSILIA. Perhaps. But you must help me. You must, you must.
Make me *her.*

LUDOVICO. Make you – ?

ERSILIA. Make me into that woman that you imagined. If I could
only be that *me* you gave my story to . . . I feel so cheated by
that.

LUDOVICO *laughs.*

LUDOVICO. You feel robbed?

ERSILIA. I *have* been. I wanted to end my life. And I think my
unhappiness has earned me . . . I shouldn't be saying this . . .
I'm nothing . . . but nothings have rights, I'm sure of it, and
what I've done, and what's been done to me, has earned me the
right to exist. If nowhere else, then in your story. Put me into
it, please! I'd treasure it. Your books are beautiful. What you
wrote in . . . what was it called? 'The Outsider'. No. 'The One
Outside'.

LUDOVICO. 'The One Outside' is nothing to do with me.

ERSILIA. Didn't you write it?

LUDOVICO. No.

ERSILIA. I thought you . . .

LUDOVICO. No. In fact it's by a man whom I particularly
dislike.

ERSILIA. Oh God . . . !

LUDOVICO. Though any praise is welcome.

*She covers her face with her hands.*

Don't cry. Oh, this is dreadful.

*She goes on crying.*

You must have read some genuine book of mine and confused
the titles.

ERSILIA. No . . . everything I do is hopeless.

*There's a knock at the door.*

LUDOVICO. Who's that?

SIGNORA ONORIA *comes in, emanating charm.*

ONORIA. May I come in?

*She peers round the room, looking for* ERSILIA.

Where is she?

*She stops and places her hands together in compassion.*

Why is she crying?

LUDOVICO (*surprised at this unannounced change of mood*).
What do you want?

ONORIA. You might have said our guest was a celebrity!
Signorina Drei? Yes? The lady in the news? Ah, look, the roses
are back in your cheeks!

LUDOVICO. How did you know it was she?

ONORIA. Do you think that nobody else can read?

LUDOVICO (*sharp*). How did you know that *this* young lady was
the woman you'd read about?

ONORIA. Your visitor told me.

*And she hands him a visiting card.*

Here's his card.

LUDOVICO. Who is he?

ONORIA. A journalist.

LUDOVICO. Is he outside? What does he want?

ONORIA. To see the young lady.

LUDOVICO. How did he know she was here?

*To* ERSILIA.

Did you . . . ?

ERSILIA. How could I tell him? I didn't know where I would be.

LUDOVICO. I see.

*To* ERSILIA, *with an eloquent glance at* ONORIA.

He must have heard it on Amphibian Radio. Will you speak to
him?

ERSILIA. What does he want?

LUDOVICO. Let's see.

*He goes out.*

ONORIA. Poor child! I've never cried so much as when I read
your story in the paper.

ERSILIA. I thought they'd leave me alone now.

ONORIA. No, they never give up. How do you feel?

ERSILIA. I'm ill. It's here.

*She indicates her chest.*

I can't breathe. The hospital let me go too early. I've recovered
from the poison. But there's something else. I'm shaking. Oh
God!

*A barrel organ is heard from the street.*

ONORIA. Unbutton your blouse.

ERSILIA. No! Send him away!

ONORIA *takes out her purse and goes to the window. Opens it and shouts.*

ONORIA. . You!

*She takes a couple of coins from her purse and throws them down.*

Someone is ill up here! Move on!

*The song stops abruptly in mid-bar.* ONORIA *closes the window. Turns back.*

He's gone now.

*She glances at the bedroom.*

Quick, get into bed before the journalist finds you.

ERSILIA. I can't. I must be ready to go. This can't last. I know it can't.

ONORIA. *What* can't?

ERSILIA. *This!* All *this*! Oh, it's too tight . . . !

*She loosens her belt.*

Help me . . . !

LUDOVICO *is heard inviting someone to step inside.*

LUDOVICO. After you.

ALFREDO CANTAVALLE, *a journalist, comes in, followed by* LUDOVICO.

CANTAVALLE. May I come in?

*He sees* ERSILIA.

Ah, Signorina Drei. You've not forgotten me?

LUDOVICO. This is Alfredo Cantavalle, journalist.

ERSILIA. We met before.

CANTAVALLE (*pleased*). You remember? I'm flattered.

*Of* ONORIA.

And would this lady be a relative?

LUDOVICO. Signora Onoria owns the building.

CANTAVALLE. I'm honoured to meet you.

*He bows.*

The young lady had described herself as being alone in the world. But I couldn't help asking.

*To* ONORIA.

That was a nasty accident on your doorstep. Were you very upset?

ONORIA. Terribly, terribly.

LUDOVICO. An elderly man was injured.

CANTAVALLE. Killed.

ONORIA. Is he dead?

CANTAVALLE. He died in the ambulance.

LUDOVICO. Who was he?

CANTAVALLE. Nobody knows. May I . . . ?

*He turns to* ERSILIA.

Allow me, dear lady, to congratulate you on your good fortune. I'm sure you won't mind my claiming some of the credit. It was my article, I think, which stirred the heart of this distinguished man of letters?

*To* LUDOVICO.

A magnificent gesture, Maestro. It really is one of those moments when one feels proud to be a journalist.

ERSILIA. I'm very grateful.

LUDOVICO. I have nothing to say. I abhor publicity, and I . . .

CANTAVALLE. But you'll stay and listen? I'd be so grateful for your comments.

*To* ONORIA.

Sadly, this is a private affair.

*Unwillingly,* ONORIA *prepares to leave. To* LUDOVICO.

ONORIA. Look after her.

LUDOVICO. She's better now.

ONORIA. Look at her!

LUDOVICO (*to* ERSILIA). What's happened?

ERSILIA. I'm feverish.

CANTAVALLE (*snide*). I'm sure that if she's paid enough attention . . .

LUDOVICO. If she's not *disturbed* . . . !

ONORIA (*to* ERSILIA). Call if you want me.

ERSILIA *nods her head in thanks.*

CANTAVALLE (*to* ONORIA). Good day.

ONORIA *goes.* LUDOVICO *makes sure the door is closed behind her. Then.*

CANTAVALLE. That story of mine was an immense success. There's just one problem. It doesn't stand up.

LUDOVICO. According to whom?

CANTAVALLE. The consul.

ERSILIA. Is he in Rome?

CANTAVALLE. He is. He visited the paper yesterday and demanded a retraction.

ERSILIA. Oh God!

LUDOVICO (*to* CANTAVALLE). What *precisely* does he want retracted?

CANTAVALLE. Every word.

ERSILIA (*to* CANTAVALLE). I told you not to say his name.

CANTAVALLE. I didn't.

ERSILIA. You said the town. You said his title . . .

LUDOVICO. He can't want every *syllable* retracted.

CANTAVALLE. Pardon me, Maestro . . .

*He turns to* ERSILIA.

I promised not to mention him by name. And so I didn't.

LUDOVICO. You made the most of her naivete.

CANTAVALLE. *Somebody* was naive in the extreme, but I'm beginning to think it was probably me. I was given licence to refer to 'our consul in Smyrna.' Which seemed innocuous. Our readers don't even know where Smyrna is, let alone the name of our consul there. If I'd known he was so combustible I might have put it differently. As it was, I only found out when I discovered him exploding in all directions in my editor's office.

LUDOVICO. Why did he come to Rome?

CANTAVALLE. He's recently buried his small daughter and it seems his wife's gone mad. She's been walking around with her eyes closed so she can't see the place where her daughter fell to her death.

ERSILIA. She's crazy.

CANTAVALLE. No wonder. He came here to apply for a transfer. Then he read my column and all hell broke loose. And now he's suing the paper for libel.

LUDOVICO. But what did you *say* that could possibly . . . ?

CANTAVALLE. He didn't specify. People in his position don't have to.

ERSILIA. I don't even know what you wrote.

CANTAVALLE. I wrote what you told me. I wrote with feeling, because I felt sorry for you. But I altered nothing, I misquoted nothing. It's charming in a way to hear you being so vague about my accuracy, but if you doubt it, why don't you read the piece for yourself.

LUDOVICO *looks for it.*

LUDOVICO. I've got it somewhere.

CANTAVALLE. Don't exert yourself. I'll send a copy round by messenger.

*To* ERSILIA.

And if you can find a way of handling the consul half as well as you handled me, we'll all be grateful.

ERSILIA *leaps to her feet. In fury.*

ERSILIA. He has nothing to complain about!

CANTAVALLE. Good, we'll tell him.

ERSILIA. I'm ill. I'm ill.

*She cries.*

CANTAVALLE. Oh, please . . .

*Sobbing overwhelms her, then turns into hysterical laughter.*

LUDOVICO. Ersilia! No!

*He and* LUDOVICO *and* CANTAVALLE *cluster around. She collapses.*

LUDOVICO. Quick, call the signora.

CANTAVALLE *runs to the door and calls.*

CANTAVALLE. Signora! Signora!

LUDOVICO. Come at once please!

CANTAVALLE. Signora!

*He goes out.*

LUDOVICO. Can you hear me? Can you? It'll be all right.

*CANTAVALLE comes back bringing* ONORIA: *she has a bottle of smelling-salts in her hand.*

ONORIA. I'm here, I'm here! Poor child! Hold up her head. Like this!

*She holds the smelling salts under* ERSILIA'*s nose.*

I told you not to upset her.

CANTAVALLE. She's coming round.

LUDOVICO. We'll take her into the bedroom.

ONORIA. Don't move her!

LUDOVICO. Ersilia?

ONORIA. Can you get up?

LUDOVICO. Gently.

ERSILIA *speaks with an oddly childish voice.*

ERSILIA. Did I fall?

LUDOVICO. No, no.

ONORIA. Try to stand up.

LUDOVICO. Easy . . .

ERSILIA. I thought I was falling. I felt my body was made of lead.

*She sees* CANTAVALLE *and reacts with terror. Clambers clumsily to her feet.*

No!

*She seems about to collapse once more.* LUDOVICO *and* ONORIA *support her.*

LUDOVICO. What is it?

ERSILIA. Let me go!

ONORIA. We'll take her in there.

*She leads* ERSILIA – *with* LUDOVICO *ineffectually supporting* – *towards the bedroom.*

LUDOVICO. You'll be all right.

ONORIA. We're going to sleep now.

ERSILIA. Where are my hands . . . ? I can't feel my hands.

ONORIA *blocks the doorway to the bedroom, keeping*
LUDOVICO *out.*

ONORIA. You stay here.

*She leaves with* ERSILIA. LUDOVICO *turns to*
CANTAVALLE.

LUDOVICO. Thank you! My home invaded. And my guest in a
state of collapse. Don't you think she's suffered enough?

CANTAVALLE. This is nothing. There's a scandal about to break.
Do you remember the young lieutenant?

LUDOVICO. Yes. Laspiga. What about him?

CANTAVALLE. When his fiancée read my story, she was so
appalled by his behaviour that she broke off the engagement.

LUDOVICO. Good. I hope he's learned his lesson.

CANTAVALLE. In fact, the following morning . . . when she saw
the trousseau and the invitations . . . this was a grand society
wedding. Eight hundred guests.

LUDOVICO. Never mind that. What happened?

CANTAVALLE. She changed her mind. She said she'd marry him
after all.

LUDOVICO. Then the scandal's been averted.

CANTAVALLE. No, it's worse than ever. Laspiga won't take her
back.

LUDOVICO. The man's a scoundrel!

CANTAVALLE. He's repentant! He's remorseful! The girl he left
behind has tried to poison herself in a public park. So now he
loves her more than ever!

LUDOVICO. How do you know?

CANTAVALLE. The consul told me. The fiancée went to see him,
and she . . .

LUDOVICO. Are we seriously to trust the word of a jilted woman
and a man who blames our friend for the death of his child?

CANTAVALLE. I don't know *who* to trust.

LUDOVICO. Then may I suggest the course of prudence. Give this
young woman the peace and quiet she needs for her
recuperation. Give the lieutenant time for a change of heart.
And as for the consul . . . tell him to go to hell!

FRANCO LASPIGA *appears abruptly at the open door. He's twenty-seven, blond and fashionably-dressed, but dishevelled after several sleepless nights.*

FRANCO. Excuse me, gentlemen! Where is she?

LUDOVICO. Who are you?

FRANCO. I'm Franco Laspiga. I'm the man who –

LUDOVICO. Yes I've . . . (*heard all about* you!)

FRANCO. I went to the hospital, but she'd gone. So I ran to the newspaper office, and they told me . . . one moment, please.

*To* CANTAVALLE.

Forgive me. Are you Ludovico Nota?

CANTAVALLE. Over there.

LUDOVICO (*bristling*). That's me. But how did my name get involved in this?

CANTAVALLE. Maestro, you are a public figure . . .

LUDOVICO *throws his hands in the air.*

LUDOVICO. This is unbearable!

CANTAVALLE. You can't pull a stunt like this and expect people not to talk about it.

FRANCO. A *stunt?*

LUDOVICO. Nothing could be further from my mind than stunts or shows or public spectacles . . . !

FRANCO. *Isn't she here?*

CANTAVALLE. Then what do you want?

FRANCO. Where *is* she?

LUDOVICO (*furious*). I want this interest in myself to stop! I think it's morbid.

*He turns to* FRANCO.

She arrived here less than an hour ago.

FRANCO. Where is she?

LUDOVICO. I picked her up . . . I *met* her, *met* her at the hospital. As she had nowhere to stay, I offered her the shelter of these lodgings. Naturally I shall sleep in a hotel.

FRANCO. Thank you, Maestro. I greatly appreciate your generosity.

LUDOVICO (*irritated*). Yes, we old men have our uses, I suppose? Why are you looking for her?

FRANCO. I want to throw myself at her feet! I want to beg her forgiveness!

CANTAVALLE. The act of a gentleman.

LUDOVICO. Though it's taken him half the week to make his mind up.

FRANCO. I was in agony! The days went . . . (*by*)! Where is she? Through that door? Let me see her!

LUDOVICO. Certainly not. It would be catastrophic.

FRANCO. In the name of pity!

CANTAVALLE. Shouldn't we warn her?

LUDOVICO. Out of the question! She's gone to bed.

FRANCO. Hasn't she recovered?

LUDOVICO. Recovered? No! She fainted only moments ago.

CANTAVALLE. The maestro's view is that we should avoid excitement. If you . . .

FRANCO. I woke up to find my life in ruins. Newspaper-boys were shouting my name. My engagement was a farce. Neighbours whispering on the stairs. Then this morning, I went to the hospital. The bed was empty. I felt I'd murdered her. I felt like a stupid, brutal, mindless oaf who kills things by stamping on them. I have to see her! I have to make things better!

ONORIA *comes out of the bedroom. She quickly closes the door behind her.*

ONORIA. Quiet, for the love of heaven! She's listening.

FRANCO. Does she know I'm here?.

ONORIA. Of course! Imagine how she feels! Don't go in! She'll throw herself out the window.

FRANCO. Can't she forgive me?

CANTAVALLE (*to* ONORIA). He's in despair.

ONORIA. She has renounced you.

LUDOVICO (*with interest*). Has she?

ONORIA (*to* FRANCO). She will not break the heart of an innocent woman.

FRANCO. What?

ONORIA. She wants you to return to your fiancée.

FRANCO. This is absurd. I don't have a fiancée. And the woman I love is through that door.

ONORIA. That's not what *she* says.

FRANCO. But I'm here to say how sorry I am, and . . .

ONORIA. Not so loud! You mustn't disturb her.

FRANCO (*to* LUDOVICO). Can't you talk to her?

LUDOVICO. Certainly, certainly.

FRANCO. Tell her the past is past. And this is our chance to make up for it.

LUDOVICO. Anything else?

FRANCO. Just go!

LUDOVICO *goes into the bedroom.*

ONORIA. He can't help you. It's the other woman.

FRANCO. But there *is* no other woman. She . . . in there . . . and I had a moment of absolute truth.

CANTAVALLE (*murmurs quietly*) 'My Night of Love.'

FRANCO. That's what it was. I'll never forget the things I said to her. It's just that . . . after I left . . . none of them seemed quite real.

CANTAVALLE. 'Love Rat Retracts'.

FRANCO. It's true. I can't excuse it. Well, I can in a way. I felt that she and I . . . and the sound of the sea, and . . . all the rest of it . . . were like a dream. Better than life, but not so pressing. So when her letters arrived, I'd think 'Oh what's that thrilling, romantic, dreamlike letter doing on my humdrum doormat?' and I'd put it in a drawer and try not to think about it. That's why the shock was so appalling when I opened the paper and saw her name in print. She was suddenly . . . real. I felt that my heart would jump out of my chest. I thought I would die.

LUDOVICO *comes back. He carries a clean shirt, socks, handkerchief and one or two other overnight things, and wears a look of grim satisfaction.*

FRANCO. Well?

LUDOVICO. No visitors.

*He starts packing a small suitcase.*

FRANCO. And?

LUDOVICO. She may be well enough tomorrow.

FRANCO. For pity's sake . . . I've not slept for three nights. Let me say just one word to her.

LUDOVICO. Wait till the morning.

FRANCO. Why?

LUDOVICO. I'll have put a word in for you.

FRANCO. But it said in the paper that she tried to kill herself because of me. Why won't she see me now?

LUDOVICO *becomes irate.*

LUDOVICO. I can't imagine! But she will in time!

CANTAVALLE. When you've both calmed down.

FRANCO. I can't.

LUDOVICO. Well that's what's happening!

*To* ONORIA, *who is half-invisible in the gloom.*

Signora . . .

*He sees her.*

Will you go to her please?

ONORIA. Put on the lights. It's like a tomb in here.

*She goes out towards the bedroom.* LUDOVICO *has finished packing.*

LUDOVICO. Gentlemen, I'm leaving.

FRANCO. Can't I . . . ?

LUDOVICO. No! Tomorrow!

*With bitterness.*

When your youthful ardour will no doubt sweep all before it.

*He clicks the catches of his suitcase with an air of decision. To* CANTAVALLE.

Shall we . . . ?

*They start to go.* CANTAVALLE *says quietly to* LUDOVICO.

CANTAVALLE. She takes him back, the story's dead, and the consul gets bored and goes back to Smyrna.

LUDOVICO. Who can say?

FRANCO. I hoped that my arrival . . .

LUDOVICO (*to* CANTAVALLE). After you.

CANTAVALLE. Thank you.

LUDOVICO (*to* FRANCO). Your arrival? *That* would make her better I suppose? 'The cure that kills.'

*They are gone. The stage remains empty for a moment. We hear the sounds of the street. Then the door from the bedroom opens and* ERSILIA *emerges.* ONORIA *enters after her.*

ONORIA. It's crazy! You can't go now.

ERSILIA. I will. I'll vanish into the street.

*She's putting on her hat.*

ONORIA. I won't let you.

ERSILIA. Let me go!

ONORIA. But what's the matter?

ERSILIA. I don't want people talking about me. I don't want to see them.

ONORIA. Not even the lieutenant?

ERSILIA. No!

ONORIA. Fine! Nobody's going to force you.

ERSILIA. I thought no-one would find me here!

ONORIA. They won't. We'll send them away.

ERSILIA. It won't work. He'll get sick of me.

ONORIA. Signor Nota? No! He has his funny ways, but he's a good fellow at heart.

ERSILIA. But there's the other.

ONORIA. Who?

ERSILIA. I don't want to say his name.

ONORIA. The consul?

ERSILIA. Yes! Oh God, let me go!

ONORIA. Quietly, my darling! Signor Nota won't take any nonsense from that old fool.

*ERSILIA collapses on to a chair.*

Look at you!

ERSILIA. What am I to do?

ONORIA. Go back to bed. I'll make you something. Then you'll sleep.

ERSILIA *turns to her shyly. Confides, woman-to-woman.*

ERSILIA. But all I've got is what I arrived with.

ONORIA. So?

ERSILIA. I had a suitcase at the hotel. But I don't know where it's got to. Perhaps they took it to pay the rent.

ONORIA. We'll send for it tomorrow. Or I'll collect it myself. Now go to bed.

ERSILIA. I can't! That's what I'm trying to tell you. I've nothing to sleep in.

ONORIA (*affectionately*). Don't worry. No-one will see you. Go to bed. Go on!

*She goes. ERSILIA sits for a moment, looking round the room. Then, exhausted, she droops her head to one side. Breathes with difficulty, feels her icy forehead: she's afraid she'll faint again.*

*She gets up, goes to the window. It's evening now: the street is quieter.*

*A group of young men passes below. One of them is singing a sentimental song: 'Mimosa'. He tries to reach a high note, but muffs it. Jeers and derision from his friends.*

ERSILIA *returns to her seat at the table. The footsteps of the young men fade into the distance. Her eyes are wide and staring, her voice a mere whisper.*

ERSILIA. The street . . .

*End of Act One.*

## Act Two

*The following morning.* FRANCO *and* LUDOVICO NOTA *come in, followed by* EMMA, *the maid.*

LUDOVICO. Is the Signora here?

    EMMA *indicates the bedroom door.*

EMMA. She's in the bedroom.

LUDOVICO. Did the young lady sleep well?

EMMA. She was up and about all night. The signora didn't sleep a wink.

FRANCO. I knew I should have stayed.

LUDOVICO (*to* EMMA). Go in, as quietly as you can, and tell the Signora that we're here.

    EMMA *nods. As she goes.*

Has the post arrived?

EMMA. It's there on the desk.

    *She opens the bedroom door without a sound and is gone.*

LUDOVICO. You'd better sit down.

FRANCO. I can't.

    LUDOVICO *sniffs the stale air of the room. Goes over to the window: opens it. Looks at his post: it's mostly junk mail. Also a couple of newspapers, delivered by hand that morning. He glances at a newspaper, then shows it to* FRANCO, *a finger pressed against the relevant item.*

LUDOVICO. Look at this.

FRANCO. A retraction?

LUDOVICO. It seems a fuller version will appear tomorrow.

    FRANCO *reads the newspaper piece. There's a noise from the street.* LUDOVICO *strides over to the window and closes it.*

    *Meanwhile,* ONORIA *comes in from the bedroom, followed by* EMMA, *who passes through the room and goes out.*

ONORIA. What a night!

FRANCO. Is she awake?

ONORIA. She is. She knows you're here. But please, I beg, no shouting this time. She didn't sleep till after sunrise.

LUDOVICO. That's a wonder, with the market starting up.

ONORIA (*to* FRANCO). She woke when the maid came in. I was afraid she might refuse to see you.

FRANCO. And?

ONORIA. She will.

FRANCO. Thank God for that. I'm certain that once we're face to face . . .

LUDOVICO. . . . all three of us . . .

ONORIA. Don't count on anything. After you left last night she tried to run away.

LUDOVICO. To *what?*

FRANCO. Where was she going?

ONORIA. Who knows? I had to hold her down. The hospital should never have let her go.

LUDOVICO. Nonsense! When it was only she and I . . .

ONORIA. Oh, what do you know? She's in a terrible state. But she's frightened to show it. She thinks you'll get bored with her.

LUDOVICO. Hardly bored. (*To* FRANCO.) And *you* can . . .

FRANCO. She'll be fine.

ONORIA. There's one more thing. She wants her suitcase. It's at the hotel. Or perhaps the police have taken it. Someone will have to collect it for her.

LUDOVICO (*prevaricates*). We'll see about that.

ONORIA. She wants it now! She's hasn't anything to . . . (*wear*). She wants to look her best.

FRANCO. I'll get it.

ONORIA. It would be more proper if Signor Nota went.

LUDOVICO. I'm sure between us . . . and she's getting up now?

ONORIA. She is. Be nice to her.

LUDOVICO. That's ironic, coming from you. It's only yesterday that . . .

ONORIA. Yesterday I didn't know! God in heaven, to see her now . . . ! Exhausted, frightened . . . !

LUDOVICO. So you're converted. Good. I must confess to a certain exasperation. I had a story in mind. And every time that door flies open it gets mangled. First that hack. Then Casanova here. And now the Consul's racketing round the newspaper office demanding rewrites . . .

FRANCO. Is Grotti in Rome?

LUDOVICO. Of course! Come one, come all! He's even been waylaid by your fiancée.

FRANCO. What did she want?

LUDOVICO. A sympathetic audience, I imagine.

FRANCO. No, she's cleverer than that. She's going to make him twist my arm.

LUDOVICO. Yes, very likely! As I was saying . . . I plucked a tale from life, and peopled it with my imagination. The last thing I needed was a set of heavy-handed interruptions from the source material. It's quite spoiled it for me. Still, you're here now.

FRANCO (*with confidence*). Yes.

ONORIA. I'm going to sleep.

*She makes an imploring gesture.*

Be gentle with her!

*She goes.*

FRANCO. I'm going to take her away. *Really* away. To some exotic place, where nobody knows her.

LUDOVICO. Let's not be rash.

FRANCO. I'm only thinking of her happiness.

LUDOVICO. Then may I suggest that you avoid impulsive gestures? They've done her nothing but harm in the past, as you should know.

FRANCO. You're wrong. What harmed her was when I acted sensibly. When I turned away from the sea and waded back into the grey mediocrity of middle-class life. You wouldn't understand.

LUDOVICO. Because I'm old? But I'm an artist. I know those moments when the soul takes wing.

FRANCO. You do?

LUDOVICO. Oh yes. When one's spirit soars above the petty cares of everyday existence. And the chains which bind one are miraculously dissolved. But it passes.

FRANCO. Only because the soul gives up.

LUDOVICO. The soul, dear boy, has a will of its own. It's like a mischievous child. It's happy to dart about above the clouds. It loves to play. But then comes supper-time. And as the sun sinks low, a small but remorseless hand will drag you home.

FRANCO. It isn't the soul that drags us home. It's us. Ourselves. Our fears, our cowardice. I ran away from her. I lost my soul. Well, now I've found it again. In her.

LUDOVICO. Wait till you see her.

FRANCO. I'll bring her back.

*The door to the bedroom opens.* ERSILIA *enters. She looks exhausted and dishevelled. Her hair is loose, her face is pale. At the sight of her,* FRANCO *lowers his voice.*

Oh God.

ERSILIA *goes to* LUDOVICO. *Desperate, decisive.*

ERSILIA. I can't stay here. What you've offered me . . . it's too generous. I can't accept it.

LUDOVICO *indicates* FRANCO.

LUDOVICO. But look who's come to meet you.

FRANCO. Ersilia!

ERSILIA. Yes?

*Pause*

Well? What do you see?

FRANCO. I can see you've suffered. But you're still mine.

*He tries to touch her: she recoils.*

ERSILIA. Don't touch me!

*She moves away. He waits.*

I want you to go now. It's over.

FRANCO. But I've come back.

ERSILIA. What you were can never come back.

FRANCO. Look at me! I'm the same as I always was!

ERSILIA. Not me. I'm different.

FRANCO. Were you different when you tried to kill yourself?

ERSILIA. That was nothing to do with you.

FRANCO. You said it was. It said in the paper that you . . .

ERSILIA. I thought I was dying. I *wanted* to die. So I gave them a reason and they believed it. I even believed it myself at the time.

FRANCO. Then why not now?

ERSILIA. Because sadly I'm still alive.

FRANCO. How can you say that? It's a miracle.

ERSILIA. I didn't ask for a miracle. Not that one. You're mixing me up with the woman I tried to kill. Maybe she was the kind who dies for love. I don't know. And I'm not interested. She's irrelevant.

FRANCO. So I *was* the reason . . . !

ERSILIA. *Was!* I wanted to finish it! End it! But I *didn't* end it! So it doesn't matter!

FRANCO. I can bring you back to life!

ERSILIA. You can't! You can't!

FRANCO. If you wanted to kill yourself because I'd left you . . . which is what you said . . . and what I believe . . . then your reason to die is now a reason to live! I'm here now.

ERSILIA*'s manner changes: her voice is sharp and staccato, her hands jabbing at each word.*

ERSILIA. *Who* is?

FRANCO. I don't understand.

ERSILIA *throws her hands in the air, then suddenly crosses the room and sits. The two men watch in consternation: it's as though she's been transformed into a different person before their eyes. Silence for a moment. Then, in her usual tone.*

ERSILIA. Do you sometimes feel you hardly recognise me?

FRANCO. No.

ERSILIA. That's strange. If I'd seen you before I tried . . . I would never have said . . . that you were the reason. It would be impossible. I look at you now. Are your eyes the same? I can't tell. Your voice is different. But perhaps it's only different from the voice I imagined. I don't know what I imagined.

FRANCO. You're making this up. I don't believe it.

ERSILIA. That's because you don't know what it's like when your life comes back . . . not gently, from inside you, like memories do . . . but suddenly, out of the dark. It's like finding an intruder in your bedroom. Or being attacked by a stranger. Because there's *nothing* that's familiar. I search and search for something I can recognise . . . but it's hopeless. Because I've changed too. I've changed from being no more than a young man's vision of me. Tell me the truth. Am I really the same?

FRANCO. You've changed. You never used to talk like this. That speech you've just made was . . . (*incomprehensible*).

ERSILIA. . . . true! It was true. When I tell you to go, *that's* true as well. I don't know why you're staying. You could walk out of that door and no-one would blame you. Why don't you? Go! It isn't your fault!

FRANCO. *What* isn't?

ERSILIA. What you did.

FRANCO. How can it not be mine? Why do you think I'm here? Why do you think I'm begging you for forgiveness?

ERSILIA. Apologies come cheap.

FRANCO. I'm not acting out of duty. This is remorse. It's repentance. It's misery at the harm I've done you.

ERSILIA. What if I'm not the woman you thought?

FRANCO *is disturbed by her tone.*

FRANCO. What do you mean?

ERSILIA *indicates* LUDOVICO.

ERSILIA. Just as I wasn't the woman that *he* thought, either.

*She turns to* LUDOVICO.

Though I wish I could be. I'd give the whole of the nothing I have, if I could only live on in the glow of your imagination. But the life I tried to leave wouldn't let me go. It sank its teeth into me and it clenched its jaws . . .

*She stops. At the point of breakdown.*

Oh, what can I do?

LUDOVICO (*quickly, to* FRANCO). She needs to rest. Once she's recovered, she'll be . . .

ERSILIA (*to* LUDOVICO). Don't! You're driving me mad!

LUDOVICO (*dismayed*). But what have I . . . ?

ERSILIA. This is impossible. Can't you see that?

LUDOVICO. Why?

ERSILIA. You know! You said your artist's intuition told you. You hugged yourself with delight. Did you ever think that what you imagined was something I had to go down an alley and *do*?

*Pause*

Tell him. Then he'll go.

LUDOVICO. You weren't to blame.

ERSILIA. I'll tell him myself.

*To* FRANCO.

I went into the street, and I offered myself to the first man who'd take me.

FRANCO *covers his face with his hands.*

LUDOVICO. She was desperate.

FRANCO *nods.*

LUDOVICO. She was penniless. She couldn't even pay for her room. It was the day before she . . . (*tried to kill herself*). Do you understand?

FRANCO (*to* ERSILIA, *his eyes averted*). It makes me even worse than I thought.

*He looks at her.*

I'll make it up to you.

ERSILIA. Don't!

FRANCO. But it's . . . (*my responsibility*).

ERSILIA. Shall I tell you about it? Shall I tell you what I can hardly admit to myself?

*She stops to collect herself. Then.*

I worked out how I would feel. I measured it. This much need against that much disgust. I powdered my face, and then I left the hotel with a small tube of poison in my handbag. I had two of them. They were meant as disinfectant. So: poison, powder, lipstick . . . no, first a long look in the mirror which stood on the dressing-table. I did the same the following day. The day that I chose the poison. Except that *then*, when I left the hotel, I still hadn't quite decided. I sat on the bench in the park. I was wearing make-up. I had my favourite dress on . . . this one, but it was clean and pressed. And the choice was clear. This much death against that much prostitution. And I *still* didn't know . . . (*which to choose*). If a man had sat next to me . . . someone attractive . . . or with time on his hands . . . Do you see what I'm saying? Do you understand now why I'm here? A man who knew nothing about me offered me shelter. And I accepted. Selling myself is easy now. I've found the knack.

FRANCO. I know why you're talking like this. Why you're degrading yourself . . .

ERSILIA. It isn't *me* who's . . . (*degrading me*).

FRANCO. Very well then! If it's other people . . . if it's me who dragged you into the mud . . . which it is, I know . . . why won't you let me help you?

ERSILIA. By degrading me all the more?

FRANCO. No! Never! By . . . (*taking you away to a new life!*)

ERSILIA *hammers out each word of her answer.*

ERSILIA. I am a liar. I am a fraud. Not a word of truth has passed my lips as long as I can remember. None of this has anything to do with you. It's life. That's all. It's a life that drags on and on and on and amounts to nothing.

EMMA *comes in.*

EMMA. The Signor Consul Grotti is waiting outside.

ERSILIA. I knew it.

LUDOVICO. Who does he want?

FRANCO. I'll speak to him.

EMMA. He only wants to speak to the Signorina.

ERSILIA. Let him come in.

EMMA *goes.*

It would be best if I saw him alone.

GROTTI *comes in. He's dark, robust. Late thirties. Habitual expression of hard, unyielding restraint. Formal, black suit.*

Consul Grotti.

*To* GROTTI.

May I present Signor Ludovico Nota.

GROTTI *bows.*

GROTTI. I know the name.

ERSILIA. The Maestro has been kind enough to lend me his lodgings.

*She indicates* FRANCO.

Signor Laspiga . . . (*you know*).

FRANCO. We met in happier circumstances. But . . .

ERSILIA. Don't talk.

FRANCO. I have something to say.

ERSILIA. Not now. I want you to go. I want nothing more to do with you. How many times must I tell you?

FRANCO *holds up a hand for silence.*

FRANCO. One moment. (*To* GROTTI.) You see before you the woman I intend to marry . . .

ERSILIA. Be quiet!

FRANCO. . . . and I request the Signor Consul to repeat that sentence word for word to the person who sent him.

ERSILIA. Have you gone mad?

FRANCO. Surely you know that he's met with my fiancée?

*In great consternation,* ERSILIA *turns to* GROTTI.

ERSILIA. Did you talk about me?

GROTTI *is calm and composed.*

GROTTI. I merely promised that I would call.

FRANCO. Nothing you say will affect my decision.

ERSILIA *speaks to* FRANCO *with a hint of imperious anger.*

ERSILIA. I wish to discuss this alone with the Signor Consul.

*In a softer tone, to* LUDOVICO.

If you . . . (*wouldn't mind leaving*)?

FRANCO. I have more to say . . . !

*To* GROTTI.

Whatever this young lady decides . . .

*He indicates* ERSILIA.

. . . the course I have chosen to take will remain unaltered. My fiancée rejected me in the sharpest terms. And she was right to do so. It is a matter for regret that, rather than stand by that, she seeks to change my mind.

*To both* ERSILIA *and* GROTTI.

Whatever the two of you agree, I shall follow my conscience.

*To* LUDOVICO.

I'm sure I have your support.

LUDOVICO. You do.

FRANCO. Good day.

GROTTI. Good day.

LUDOVICO (*quietly to* ERSILIA). I'll see to your suitcase.

ERSILIA. Thank you.

LUDOVICO (*to* GROTTI). Good day to you.

GROTTI *nods politely.* FRANCO *and* LUDOVICO *go. Once the door has closed behind them and their footsteps have died away.*

GROTTI. You cunt. You dim little cunt. Why did you lie?

ERSILIA. It was true. I tried to kill myself.

GROTTI. But why did you say it was because of him? To get him back?

ERSILIA. No! Didn't you hear what I said?

GROTTI. He didn't believe you. Was he meant to?

ERSILIA. Yes! I can't *make* him believe it. He's greedy for guilt. He can't get enough of it.

GROTTI. You have the audacity to talk about other people's guilt!

ERSILIA. Do you think it's only me who ought to feel guilty? At least I had the courage to die.

GROTTI. Do you think I should have cut my throat in a fit of repentance?

ERSILIA. You know nothing. You with your cosy life and your steady income. All that time I was planning my death, not one thought of guilt crossed my mind. I was alone and hungry and thrown out naked into the street. And I still felt strong.

GROTTI. So you lied.

ERSILIA. I had good reason. He'd promised to marry me.

GROTTI. He was joking.

ERSILIA. No. He meant what he said, and when he got home he went back on it, like the little mummy's boy he is. He didn't even know about you and me, so he can't use that as an excuse.

GROTTI. Neither can you. Under the circumstances. But it didn't stop you lying.

ERSILIA. How can you compare it? He'd got engaged. He'd announced his wedding!

GROTTI. He had sex before marriage. Men do that. It just so happened that the sex was you.

ERSILIA. He was serious. He's serious now. You're just trying to justify what you did to me when his back was turned.

GROTTI. So to ruin his marriage, you created a public scandal.

ERSILIA. No.

GROTTI. What would you have done if . . . when you arrived in Rome . . . you'd found that he was free to marry you?

ERSILIA (*with great emphasis*). I would never have deceived him. I swear on the soul of your child. I didn't even try to find him.

GROTTI. Although you must have made enquiries?

ERSILIA. Never.

GROTTI. Then how did you know he'd got engaged?

ERSILIA. Oh . . . they told me at the Naval Ministry.

GROTTI. Though you didn't enquire.

ERSILIA *speaks with rising fury.*

ERSILIA. You should thank me.

GROTTI. For the efforts which you made to find him?

ERSILIA. No! Because when they told me . . . all the terrible things I'd planned to do to you seemed completely stupid. You think you caught me out. You don't know what was going through my mind as I walked up the Ministry steps. I was remembering you pulling the sheets up round us. The door flung wide. Your wife, mouth open, staring down at us. The sound of a crowd in the street. A child had fallen from the roof. I climbed the steps to the Ministry with voices jabbering in my brain. Like a derelict. Like an old madwoman spilling out her life story. That's the only reason I wanted to find him. To tell him everything.

GROTTI. About us?

ERSILIA. About you.

GROTTI. And you?

ERSILIA. Do you want to know? Be careful. I've touched the bottom of the pit. I know what it's like. I can say anything now. When he left, I was hot, I was warm from the touch of his flesh. You knew it. You could smell it on my skin. You knew I'd melt at the stroke of a finger. So you took me. But I fought. I scratched your neck, I scratched your arms. Can you deny it?

GROTTI. You led me on.

ERSILIA. Not true.

GROTTI. Perhaps not the first time. But the second?

ERSILIA. No.

GROTTI. When no-one was looking you'd touch me.

ERSILIA. Never.

GROTTI. You stroked my arm with a needle.

ERSILIA. I was threatening you!

GROTTI. You were a blushing virgin. Is that what you're saying?

ERSILIA. I was your employee.

GROTTI. So you were just obeying orders?

ERSILIA. Only my body obeyed you. Not my mind. I hated you.

GROTTI. But you loved what I did. You were hungry for it. You were worse than a whore.

ERSILIA. That's what I hated most. When it was over, I'd lie there wanting to castrate you with my bare hands. I wanted to leave you raw and bleeding. I'd go into the bathroom and bite my arms till I drew blood. I'd yielded, I'd fallen, but only my body. My heart held fast to the one good thing in my life. I was going to marry the man I loved.

GROTTI. Who was getting engaged elsewhere.

ERSILIA. Yes, he was a bastard too. And you accuse me of leading you on. Merely because I haven't the wit to be . . . anything! If I threw that vase on the floor, it would still be *something*. I'm not even that. I go where I'm put, I lie where I'm thrown . . . if I could only, just once, get up on my feet and shout, 'Stop! I'm here!'

GROTTI. But that's exactly what you've done! You've plastered yourself all over the papers, you've . . . (*disrupted people's lives, etc.*).

ERSILIA. I should have crept under a stone. Is that it?

GROTTI. You might have considered that. Rather than throwing it into the mud, so that everyone who's ever had anything to do with you is splattered with filth.

ERSILIA. All right! I'll do it! I'll sink from sight! You can go back to your affairs of state. And he can . . .

GROTTI. I shall go back to wreckage. To a wife who hates me and a dead daughter. Thanks to you.

ERSILIA. It was you! That chair I took up to the roof. You told me not to bring it down. You said we hadn't got time.

GROTTI. What were you doing up there? My wife was ill. You were supposed to stay in earshot of her bedroom.

ERSILIA. I was sewing and the child was playing.

GROTTI. You were waiting for me.

ERSILIA. You would have come for me anywhere. Even outside your wife's bedroom . . .

GROTTI. No.

ERSILIA. You'd done it before.

GROTTI. I went up on to the roof because you wanted me to.

ERSILIA. Not at first. Later. After you'd bullied me, after you'd pressed yourself against me. I'd want you then. Isn't that what you like to hear? I went on to the roof so your wife wouldn't hear us. I was sitting by the railing. The child was playing. I looked down at the street and . . . yes, I'm sure of it now . . . I heard a voice telling me not to forget the chair. Not to leave it where she could climb and fall. Then you arrived. Like an animal. Pushing, insisting. And I forgot the voice. And now I dream about it. I dream about the chair. I try to move it, try to pull it away, but . . .

*She cries.* GROTTI *is silent. After a few moments.*

GROTTI. I worked all the time. But everything I did was for other people. Never myself. Because I and my job and the house I lived in and my sick, bored, querulous wife were too frustrating to think about. Then you arrived. How did I seem to you?

ERSILIA. You seemed fine.

GROTTI. The more depressed I got, the more I tried to involve myself in the lives of other people. To help them. Since I couldn't help myself. That's why, when that boy arrived, it seemed to me so important that he should fall in love with you. I used to lie awake at night thinking about it. I'd take him for long walks and tell him what a fool he'd be to lose you. When he rose to the bait, I was delighted. I didn't even mind when I discovered that you'd become his mistress. Though my wife was upset.

ERSILIA. It was my first time. I thought I might never see him again.

GROTTI. I didn't blame you. I'd have left it at that, if . . .

ERSILIA. What?

GROTTI. A few days later, at dinner, you caught my eye. A curious, sideways look. I couldn't think what it meant. And then I knew. You were wondering if my interest in your love-life was as altruistic as it seemed. Or whether, perhaps there was something else. And I suddenly understood that 'something else' was *all* it was. It was nothing to do with finding you a decent match. And it was nothing to do with him. It was desire.

ERSILIA. Not *mine.*

GROTTI. I know. But you were the cause. You saw the truth. And, in that moment, everything I'd ever believed in was destroyed. All that was left was the brute. The animal. This thing I've become. What do you think my wife sees when she looks at me? She sees my naked body with my arms around you. She sees her child lying dead in the street. Come here.

*He gestures her over to him. She doesn't go.*

I want you to cry with me. I want us to cry together over the harm we've done.

ERSILIA. Do you think I can cry any more than I've cried already?

GROTTI. You can't go on through life as though nothing had happened. You can't go back to that boy.

ERSILIA. I won't! I promise. I'll stay here. I've been offered a home.

GROTTI. You haven't been watching. He wants you to go. He and Laspiga have stitched it up between them.

ERSILIA. But I've refused Laspiga.

GROTTI. It didn't work. You can't expect a red-blooded young man to accept a woman's refusal if she gives no reason.

ERSILIA. Then I'll tell him the reason.

GROTTI. *Will* you? Even though that reason will be so repulsive
to him that everything about you will seem shabby and mean?
That your lies will be intolerable to him? That your currying
favour with the press will seem as cheap as it is? That he'll
wake up to the fact that you destroyed his marriage?

ERSILIA. I didn't mean any of that to happen. I thought I was
dying. I *told* him that. Do you want me to tell him everything?
I can't. You and I can talk, that's different. We're accomplices.
Why must he know any more than he knows already?

GROTTI. Have you any idea of the fury I felt when I read that lie?
Then the fiancée came to see me. Desperate, in tears. She told
me that the boy had left her, that he planned to go back to you.
I felt the room spinning round me. I don't know how I
controlled myself. When she'd gone, I ran to the newspaper.
I made them take back everything they'd said about me. And
my wife. Have you thought about her? Slandered as a bad
employer, a careless mother, a vindictive bitch? She was all
set to see the fiancée herself. To tell her what you'd done.
And what she'd seen. I've promised my wife that *something,*
at least, will survive your actions. I mean, the happiness of that
innocent young woman, who considered herself engaged.
I have promised my wife that the marriage will proceed.
Do you understand?

ERSILIA. Yes.

GROTTI. Well?

ERSILIA. I'll do it.

GROTTI. *What* will you do?

ERSILIA. What you've made me do.

GROTTI. Don't move.

*He moves quickly to her. Tries to embrace her.*

ERSILIA. Leave me alone.

GROTTI. Listen . . .

ERSILIA. Don't touch me.

*He stays beside her. Perhaps touches her. Gentler now than
we've ever seen him.*

GROTTI. I sometimes think that sharing grief is the same as love.

*ERSILIA pulls away. Harshly, like a challenge.*

ERSILIA. I killed your child!

GROTTI. I know.

ERSILIA. Then why don't you go?

GROTTI. I can't.

ERSILIA *moves suddenly and quickly to the window.*

What are you doing?

*She throws open the window. The noise of the street is heard very loudly. She turns back. Looks at him.*

ERSILIA. If you don't go, I'll shout.

*She waits.*

*End of Act Two.*

## Act Three

*Later that day. The sounds of the street can can be heard, more quietly now that it's evening.* SIGNORA ONORIA *is at the window talking to a neighbour in the house opposite.* EMMA *is cleaning, dusting and muttering to herself.*

ONORIA. Of course I'll tell you! You'll be the first to know. What's that?

*She listens.*

Till noon. It's never the same, though, is it? It isn't like sleeping properly. What?

*She listens.*

I can't hear you.

*Listens.*

She's out. They've both gone out. They've gone to collect her luggage. He tried to get it earlier, but they wouldn't give it to him.

EMMA (*mutters to herself*). Won't give it to *her* if they got any sense.

ONORIA (*to the neighbour*). She was worried about her suitcase . . .

EMMA (*still to herself*). What's she doing here? . . . messing us all around . . . can't bear it . . .

ONORIA *turns to* EMMA.

ONORIA. Are you talking to me?

EMMA. I don't like cleaning up this time of day. It isn't natural.

ONORIA. Ssh!

*She turns back to the window.*

Three, did you say?

*She listens. Laughs indulgently.*

And one of them was the Maestro? I could have told you that . . . no fool like an old fool . . . Who else?

*The neighbour says more.*

The lieutenant? No, I don't (*believe she kissed him*) . . . Oh, *he* kissed *her?* That I can well imagine. And what did . . . ? *Who?*

*The neighbour adds more.*

No, that I can't believe. It was a trick of the light. You won't persuade me. Somebody's calling.

*She shuts the window and turns back into the room.*

Would you believe what that wicked old gossip just told me? She said she saw three men in here and each one of them tried to kiss her.

EMMA. The consul too?

ONORIA. Exactly! Isn't that quite absurd. A man of his distinction.

EMMA. I wouldn't know about the kissing. They were shouting, though.

ONORIA. Were they? Were they really? I hope you knew better than to listen.

EMMA. I couldn't hear 'em. I was down below. All I could tell, was he was muttering this and that and she was shouting.

ONORIA. I don't blame her. I'd shout myself if I was in her position. You should see the papers. They've virtually disowned her, thanks to him.

EMMA. I think he wants to stop her going off with the lieutenant.

ONORIA. Stop her? Quite the opposite. It's she who sent the young man packing.

EMMA. What's she going to do then? Stay on here with this old goat?

ONORIA (*bridles a bit*). I very much doubt the Maestro wants her. One's seen the warning-signs. He has his work to think of. Besides, she's far too immature for him.

EMMA. She'll have to go back to the young man, then, whether she wants him or not.

ONORIA. She can't be rushed into it. He has to prove that he's reliable. It isn't enough just saying he's sorry. Though I will concede he said it very nicely.

EMMA. Oh, he meant it.

ONORIA. And there's another reason very much on her mind. She doesn't want to hurt the other woman.

EMMA. You wouldn't catch me worrying about *her*. Not if I'd drunk that poison.

ONORIA. You'd feel very differently if you yourself had felt the pain of being abandoned. That's what Signor Cantavalle called it. Did you see the headline? 'Death is the Loneliest Place.' That's why she's here. She thought she'd found a peaceful haven, poor little mite. I was standing by the door when she and the Maestro left. There was a look in her eyes I couldn't fathom. As though she couldn't see me. I asked her how she felt, and I touched her hands . . . and they were freezing cold. And she didn't reply. Just gave a funny little smile. Oh, how I shivered!

*She cocks her ear.*

Listen! That's the woman selling ribbons. Run on down and get me some of the blue. Two metres. Go! I'll stop her.

EMMA *goes.* ONORIA *goes to the window. Opens it, leans out. Shouts.*

ONORIA. Hello!

*She waves.* FRANCO LASPIGA *comes in. He looks furious and upset.*

FRANCO. May I come in?

ONORIA *closes the window.*

ONORIA. Of course! Sit down! The Signorina will be back before you know it. And the Maestro too.

*Confidentially.*

Will you take a word of advice? Don't give up. Keep fighting.

*It takes* FRANCO *a moment to get her drift. Once he has, he replies sarcastically.*

FRANCO. Oh, I'll keep fighting.

ONORIA. The Signor Consul has spoken firmly to her. She'll come round.

FRANCO. The bastard.

ONORIA. I felt much the same myself. That poor sweet child . . .

FRANCO. Child? She isn't a child. She's a whore.

ONORIA *is shaken.*

ONORIA. My God! What did you say?

*Before* FRANCO *can answer,* LUDOVICO *comes in.*

LUDOVICO. Excellent! You've arrived before me.

*To* ONORIA.

Is she not back yet?

*Still stunned,* ONORIA *glances at him.*

ONORIA. I can't . . .

*She turns back to* FRANCO.

What did you say?

LUDOVICO. Is something wrong?

FRANCO. Signor Grotti came here this morning to see his mistress.

LUDOVICO. Who?

ONORIA. His *what?*

FRANCO. His tart. His bit of skirt. Then his wife found out. So she called on my fiancée and told her the whole disgusting story.

LUDOVICO. Ersilia and her husband?

ONORIA. Her and the consul?

FRANCO. Yes. What I don't know is when it started. Was it *after* I asked her to marry me? Or before? That's what I've come to find out.

ONORIA. How will you . . . (*find out*)? Oh God! I can't go on. I'm losing my breath.

FRANCO. And that's not all. Do you know when the wife found out about them? When the baby died.

ONORIA. Oh, this is horrible, horrible.

FRANCO. She found them in bed together. They'd left the child on the roof. They didn't care. That's why she drove her out of the house like a murderess.

ONORIA. She *was* a murderess!

FRANCO. She was lucky not to go to prison. She *would* have done, if the consul hadn't been involved. And after all that . . . after she'd reduced their lives to rubble . . .

ONORIA. . . . . she had the bare-faced cheek . . .

FRANCO. . . . . to do exactly the same to me!

ONORIA. To everyone!

FRANCO. Imagine what I've gone through . . . !

LUDOVICO (*to himself*) . . . amazing story . . .

ONORIA. Parading up and down like a martyr. And that look on her face!

FRANCO. I was pilloried. Laughed at. My fiancée, screaming insults at me. I don't know how I didn't go mad.

ONORIA. That's why she said it couldn't last! She knew any minute the whole pack of lies would explode in her face. That minx! I'd like back every tear I've ever shed over her!

*To* LUDOVICO.

Well, one thing's certain. She's not staying one more night under this roof. I want her out!

LUDOVICO. One moment, please . . .

ONORIA. Why're you defending her? She's worse than a prostitute. She's brought shame on us all. I don't want to see her again. Get rid of her.

LUDOVICO. Listen, please! I want to understand this.

*To* FRANCO.

Why did the consul protest to the newspaper?

FRANCO. That's obvious.

LUDOVICO. Not to me. I find it utterly perplexing. If they were lovers, why did he not support her?

FRANCO. Because his wife is here.

ONORIA. And she'd been slandered.

LUDOVICO. Ah, that makes sense. When she arrived, she was anxious about the papers. She wanted to know what they said.

ONORIA. Because she'd lied.

LUDOVICO. Indeed, quite so . . . but are we to think she lied consistently?

FRANCO. She's the lowest, shabbiest liar imaginable.

LUDOVICO. So when she claimed that *you* were the reason for her taking poison . . . that was a lie as well?

ONORIA. To lie about *that!*

LUDOVICO (*impatient*). I'm trying to think. (*To* FRANCO.) You see . . . if *that* was a lie, it solves a mystery.

FRANCO. Which one?

LUDOVICO. Why she rejected your apologies.

FRANCO. She could hardly have accepted them.

LUDOVICO. I don't agree. She could have forgiven you graciously and convinced us all. At least for a day or two. The fact that she didn't, suggests that *that* particular lie was in some way exceptional. That she couldn't live up to it. Whereas any habitual liar would have brazened it out.

FRANCO. She had me crying like a child.

LUDOVICO. All for nothing. Or for less than you supposed. But . . .

FRANCO. And that's the best interpretation! That's assuming that the whole loathsome business started after I'd gone. What if it started before? What if my night of love was simply her night off? That's what I've come to find out.

LUDOVICO. Oh, why are you bothering? Anyone would think she *used* that lie in order to entrap you. She didn't. When you tried to get her back, she went insane. She practically threw the crockery at you.

FRANCO. And what about the lies she told that night? That *wonderful* night?

LUDOVICO. They're unimportant.

FRANCO. How can you say . . . ?

LUDOVICO. I cannot believe I'm having to spell this out. *If*, and *if* is the word, there was an element of deception in those fumbled few hours of love, it didn't harm you. Because you promptly found a far better match elsewhere.

FRANCO. My lie makes hers all right. Is that what you're saying?

LUDOVICO. I'm saying you're ill-equipped to judge it.

FRANCO. I cancelled my wedding. I didn't leave the house for three days. Then I ran all the way to the hospital . . .

LUDOVICO. Because you thought you'd killed her.

FRANCO. But I hadn't!

LUDOVICO. Exactly! What I'm saying . . .

FRANCO. Then what are you dragging it up for?

LUDOVICO. Because it's crucial. Why did she choose that lie to tell on her deathbed? If she died, it wouldn't help her. If she lived, it would be exposed in a matter of days. As has been shown. Was it a cry for help to you? Clearly not, because she doesn't want you. Was it a signal to the consul? No, because he cannot escape his wife. So what was her motive?

FRANCO. Can't you guess?

LUDOVICO. I've no idea.

ONORIA. It's staring you in the face.

LUDOVICO. That's probably why I've missed it. I'm bad at spotting the obvious.

ONORIA. It's news to me you're bad at anything.

LUDOVICO. I'm bad at most things. Haven't you noticed?

ONORIA. I was joking.

LUDOVICO. I was serious. Well?

ONORIA. The suicide failed.

LUDOVICO. And?

FRANCO. The lie was successful.

LUDOVICO. Was it? What did it get her?

FRANCO. The person she wanted.

LUDOVICO. You, do you mean? But . . .

FRANCO. You.

LUDOVICO. *Me?*

*He thinks for a moment.*

But she can't have *intended* that. We'd never met. I doubt she's read a single line I've written.

FRANCO. She wanted a writer.

LUDOVICO. *Any* writer? Any idiot with a pen?

FRANCO. I didn't say that.

LUDOVICO. But you might as well have done. She wanted a hack. A scribbler. Say it!

ONORIA. You said it yourself.

FRANCO. She wanted to be noticed. And she knew the only way she'd ever do that was in fiction. So she made up a story . . .

ONORIA. It had romance.

FRANCO. It had betrayal.

ONORIA. Heartbreak.

LUDOVICO. Sex. That's perfectly true. I liked it at once.

*He looks suddenly very happy.*

How odd. I thought she was my creation. Whereas I was hers.

ONORIA. You'd have made a good team. She could have told the lies and you could have sold them.

LUDOVICO. If there's anything more absurd than equating fiction with common-or-garden untruths, I've yet to hear it. I could pick up my pen right now, and shut my ears, and the story I wrote would have a truth and a fire and a beauty which that unfortunate creature would never have dreamed of. Think of a detail. Take the widow. Lets rooms. Hasn't been bedded for years, so she furiously resents the nubile victim. Then, discovering that the victim is a front-page story, she becomes obsessed with her. Then decides she's not a victim after all, so she throws her out. Hilarious!

ONORIA. How dare you!

LUDOVICO. How dare I turn you into a comic archetype? Good God, woman, you should be flattered!

*To* FRANCO.

Yesterday, you were glowing, excited . . .

FRANCO. How could I not be?

LUDOVICO. How indeed? It was enchanting! You were ardour incarnate. I wanted to run to my desk and write your lines for you. That is my skill, you see. I am detached. Objective. I watch the two of you mark me down as a gullible fool. It isn't accurate, but it's ironic. I enjoy that. I even enjoy the lancing of a lie. Though I feel the pain no less than you. I can use that pain. It's what I'll draw on when I write about us.

*He looks at his watch.*

I can't help wondering if she's vanished with the money.

ONORIA. *Money?*

LUDOVICO. I lent her some. They wouldn't release her suitcase till she paid her bill.

ONORIA. If she's got money in her pocket, we've seen the last of her.

FRANCO. Do you think she's gone?

LUDOVICO. I think it's in the balance. If her lie was sane and solid and explicable . . . as the two of you believe . . . we've lost her. If . . . as *I* suspect . . . the cause was more mysterious . . . she'll return. And life will provide us with an ending. Otherwise, I'll invent one.

FRANCO. Without knowing the facts?

LUDOVICO. Facts! Facts! Facts are merely what we know already. They are, by definition, what can never surprise us. Once in the mind, they form a hardened lump. They're all that survive the death of the spirit. I can believe most things but, where facts are concerned, I am a sceptic through and through.

EMMA *appears.*

EMMA. The Signor Consul Grotti is here. He wants to speak either to you, Signor, or to the young lady.

FRANCO *is all set for a confrontation.*

FRANCO. I'll deal with him.

LUDOVICO. This is my house. I'll have no fighting.

FRANCO. Then I'll ask him to step outside.

LUDOVICO. Certainly not! Stay here. And keep your mouth shut!

GROTTI *appears in the doorway. He looks drawn and agitated.* EMMA *leaves.*

GROTTI. Good evening. Is the Signorina Drei here?

ONORIA (*brusque*). She's left.

FRANCO. She's gone for good.

GROTTI. This is worse than I feared. May I ask you, Maestro . . .

LUDOVICO. Ask away! Let's throw our manners to the winds! Did I invite you here?

GROTTI. Forgive me. I need to know whether the Signorina Drei is aware that my wife . . .

FRANCO. . . . has called on my fiancée to expose the fact that . . .

GROTTI. The only thing which my wife has exposed is the state of her own mental health.

FRANCO. Are you saying she's mad?

GROTTI. I'm not obliged to tell you anything.

FRANCO. But I want some answers.

GROTTI. Perhaps you'd like my wife's psychological history? I should have brought the dossier. What would you like to know?

FRANCO. Firstly . . .

GROTTI. Stop this nonsense! Signor Nota, you will be kind enough to tell me whether Signorina Drei knows what has happened.

LUDOVICO. I don't believe she does.

GROTTI. Thank God for that.

LUDOVICO. I was with her less an hour ago. She left me to go into the hotel. She had some business there.

GROTTI. Did *you* know?

LUDOVICO. Signor Laspiga has just told me.

GROTTI. Good. At least we can tell her in a civilised fashion. Another shock would be disastrous.

LUDOVICO. So you're assuming she'll return?

GROTTI. Why do you think she won't?

FRANCO. Because we've found her out.

GROTTI. How does she know?

FRANCO. Because she's clever. She's intuitive. She's taken the money and run.

ONORIA. She's like an animal.

GROTTI. *If* she has fled, it's under the weight of an appalling accusation.

FRANCO. But is it true or false?

GROTTI. I do not have to answer that. But I trust you are enough of a gentleman to treat my silence as a denial.

FRANCO. There speaks the diplomat.

GROTTI. Shall I put it bluntly? I won't be called to account by a pompous child. You can believe whatever suits you.

FRANCO. Who cares what suits me? I want the truth.

GROTTI. And will it satisfy you? No, of course not. If I confess, you'll fly into a tantrum. If I deny it, that will leave you as the guilty party.

FRANCO. *Me?*

GROTTI. Yes, absolutely.

FRANCO. It was in your house . . . she said . . . that she was blamed for the death of the child . . . although she wasn't even there . . . because your wife had sent her out . . .

GROTTI. That never happened.

FRANCO. Was it a lie?

GROTTI. It was misleading. I forced the paper to correct it.

FRANCO. Where the hell *was* she, then, when the baby died? And where were you? You'd ruined your alibi. That's why you came round here to cook up another one with her.

GROTTI *is shaking with fury.*

GROTTI. Forgive me, Maestro.

*To* FRANCO.

Earlier today, I called at the request of your fiancée. This gentleman was present, as were you and the lady in question. She was distressed . . .

FRANCO. I was trying to make it up to her. She wouldn't let me. She said I hadn't done anything wrong. But if I hadn't, why was she so upset?

GROTTI. Because you wouldn't stop apologising! It was driving her mad. She told you over and over again, and you wouldn't stop. It was maniacal.

FRANCO. Make me look stupid if you like. I don't mind. I haven't come here to look grand or dignified. I'm here because she tried to kill herself. Because of me. You've tried out your different versions. But that's the only one that holds. Because it's what she said. It's what they printed.

GROTTI. She denied it.

FRANCO. Who made her say it in the first place? Me, I suppose?

GROTTI. I've no idea!

FRANCO. So I *could* have been the reason?

GROTTI. I don't *know* the reason.

FRANCO. Everything points to me. And my engagement. There's no other motive.

LUDOVICO. Yes there is.

FRANCO. You don't know her motive. You admitted that. You said you thought it was mysterious.

LUDOVICO. But there's something none of us have mentioned.

FRANCO (*with irony*). Oh yes . . . the evening light . . . the knowing glance . . . the customer stops and turns . . .

GROTTI. Did *she* say this?

FRANCO (*of* LUDOVICO). He guessed it.

LUDOVICO. To my shame.

FRANCO. And she confirmed it.

GROTTI. Ah.

FRANCO *changes his tone.*

FRANCO. She rented her body to a stranger. Do you honestly think I'd let her reject me after that? I'll make her take me back. I'll wrench it out of her. But I want your word of honour that your wife . . . your sad, disturbed, unhappy wife . . . was lying. Well?

*Pause.*

Tell me you weren't her lover. Neither before, nor after.

*Pause.*

Not before.

*Pause.*

Just say it. I beg you, say it.

*Pause. He's desperate.*

Just shake your head.

EMMA *appears abruptly in the doorway.*

EMMA. Signora! Oh my God . . . ! Signora!

ONORIA. What is it?

LUDOVICO. Is she here?

EMMA. She's back.

GROTTI. Where is she?

ONORIA. What is she doing?

EMMA. She's sick! I opened the door and she almost fell into my arms. Her suitcase was open . . . !

LUDOVICO. Oh God! The poison was in the suitcase!

ERSILIA *appears in the doorway. She's pale, calm, tranquil.*

ONORIA. She's here.

GROTTI *cries out.*

GROTTI. Ersilia!

LUDOVICO. Signorina . . . !

ERSILIA. It's nothing. Please don't talk. This time, it's nothing.

*With a finger on her lips, she calls for silence. Then she sways.*

GROTTI. Take her through to the bedroom.

ONORIA. At once.

LUDOVICO. Quickly, quickly.

ERSILIA. Don't touch me! Please! I beg you!

GROTTI. Take my hand. I'll lead you.

ERSILIA. No.

LUDOVICO. We'll help you. We'll be gentle. Quickly.

ONORIA. Call for an ambulance.

ERSILIA. Leave me alone! It's hopeless!

GROTTI. No, there's time.

ERSILIA. Leave me alone. There's nothing any of you can do. It's taking longer than I thought it would. But it won't be long now. Signor Nota . . . one small favour . . . ?

LUDOVICO. Whatever you want.

ERSILIA. Your bed.

LUDOVICO. At once!

ONORIA. Come. Come.

GROTTI. What have you done? What have you done?

LUDOVICO. I would have helped you. I would have given you shelter.

ERSILIA. If I had lived, no-one would ever have believed me.

FRANCO. What do you want us to believe?

ERSILIA. That I didn't tell that lie in order to live.

FRANCO. Then why? Then why did you tell it?

ERSILIA. I lied for death. It was my beautiful final moment. That was the only thing I cared about. Not him, not you. I told you so many times. Although you wouldn't listen. I didn't love you. And I didn't miss you. And I didn't want you back. Although I didn't mean to make you so unhappy.

FRANCO. But you said it was all because of me.

ERSILIA. I know. You see . . . I couldn't believe that anything
I might do . . . not even dying . . . would affect you. I thought
I wasn't important enough. I thought I was nothing. And
I wanted so much to be more than that. I wanted people to
believe me. I wanted them not to pass by. I knew all the time,
I shouldn't be making trouble for you. I hadn't the right . . .

*She glances at* GROTTI. *Then back at* FRANCO.

You know about him and me. Did his wife do that?

FRANCO. Yes.

ERSILIA. I knew she would. Why is he here? Did he come to
deny it?

FRANCO. Yes.

ERSILIA. Well . . .

*She takes a long look at him. Then she gestures with her open
hands: 'This', she's saying, 'is why the oppressed of the world
are forced to lie.'*

*Then, quietly.*

You lied too.

FRANCO. I know.

*She smiles.*

ERSILIA. I can hardly remember what happened between us.. it
was like a dream . . . it was beautiful, though. And then, when
things went wrong, you came running to find me . . . Just like
he did.

*She indicates* GROTTI.

But the reason he ran was to tell the world that there was
nothing between us. That I didn't exist.

GROTTI *cries. For the first time, her composure is shaken. She
turns to him.*

Don't cry. Please don't. I could stop you crying, if I could only
touch you.

*She turns back to* FRANCO.

You see . . . all we want from life is to be treated with respect.
And the more we're . . .

*She searches for the phrase.*

The more we're covered in filth, the more we long for
something beautiful to wear. When I saw you again, I was

wearing my prostitute's dress. I was dressed and naked. Both at once. Then I remembered that you'd given them back your beautiful uniform. So you were also naked, in a way. When I was in the street . . .

*Her face darkens at the memory.*

. . . there was mud on my legs. Mud on my breasts. Every inch of me was defiled. That's why I lied. I wanted to die in something better than squalor and filth. I wanted to turn my death into something clean and fine. So I invented a lover who'd left me. And that was you. You were my beautiful dress. As long as I'd lived, I'd never had one. Everything I'd ever worn got tattered and ripped. The dogs would bark and leap and tear it to shreds. I wanted to die in a bridal-gown. I wanted a festival of mourning. But they wouldn't allow me even that last small scrap of pretence.

This time, I'll die as I am.

I'll die stripped bare.

I'll die despised.

I'll die humiliated.

Listen! Listen! All of you! You have nothing to tell me. Nothing to give me. Tell your wife. Tell the girl you will marry . . .

. . . I died naked.

*End of play.*

## DATE DUE

|  |  |  |  |
|---|---|---|---|
|  |  |  |  |
|  |  |  |  |
|  |  |  |  |
|  |  |  |  |
|  |  |  |  |
|  |  |  |  |
|  |  |  |  |
|  |  |  |  |
|  |  |  |  |
|  |  |  |  |
|  |  |  |  |
|  |  |  |  |
|  |  |  |  |
|  |  |  |  |
|  |  |  |  |
|  |  |  |  |
|  |  |  |  |
| GAYLORD |  |  | PRINTED IN U.S.A. |

JUN '01